An Animal Family

COWS AND CALVES

By Natalie Humphrey

Gareth Stevens
PUBLISHING

Please visit our website, www.garethstevens.com. For a free color catalog of all our high-quality books, call toll free 1-800-542-2595 or fax 1-877-542-2596.

Library of Congress Cataloging-in-Publication Data

Names: Humphrey, Natalie, author.
Title: Cows and calves / Natalie Humphrey.
Description: New York : Gareth Stevens Publishing, [2021] | Series: An animal family | Includes index.
Identifiers: LCCN 2019044947 | ISBN 9781538255766 (library binding) | ISBN 9781538255742 (paperback) | ISBN 9781538255759 (6 Pack) | ISBN 9781538255773 (ebook)
Subjects: LCSH: Calves–Juvenile literature. | Cows–Development–Juvenile literature.
Classification: LCC SF197.5 .H86 2021 | DDC 636.2–dc23
LC record available at https://lccn.loc.gov/2019044947

First Edition

Published in 2021 by
Gareth Stevens Publishing
111 East 14th Street, Suite 349
New York, NY 10003

Editor: Natalie Humphrey
Designer: Katelyn E. Reynolds

Photo credits: Cover, p. 1 GaiBru Photo/Shutterstock.com; p. 5 Vicki Smith/Moment/Getty Images; pp. 7, 24 (herd) dkHDvideo/Shutterstock.com; p.9 Jeffrey Schwartz/Shutterstock.com; pp. 11, 24 (calf) Canetti/Shutterstock.com; p. 13 Creaturart Images/Shutterstock.com; p. 15 Anton Havelaar/Shutterstock.com; p. 17 Singh Virender/Shutterstock.com; p. 19 Dean Fikar/Moment Open/Getty Images; pp. 21, 24 (farmer) Hill Street Studios/DigitalVision/Getty Images; p. 23 Iakov Filimonov/Shutterstock.com.

Printed in the United States of America

Contents

A cow family
is very big.
Cows live in herds.

Herds can have over 200 cows!

Mother cows have one baby a year.

A calf is a baby cow.

They drink milk.
The milk is from
their mother.

Mothers are
very caring.
Calves stay with them
for about 8 months.

Calves love to have fun!

They play with
their family.

Cows live on a farm.
Farmers help
calves too!

They keep calves safe. They also help them grow!

Words to Know

calf

farmer

herd

Index